© by LLF Reads & LaLa Faithful, MD

All rights reserved. No part of this book, may be reproduced, stored in a retrieval system or transmitted in any form or by any means without the prior written permission of the publishers, except by a reviewer who may quote brief passages in a review to be printed in a newspaper, magazine or other journal.

First printing
This journal was designed to guide people in fasting and prayer. It is suitable for any level of spiritual experience. It was created to build spiritual confidence and growth.

The author and publisher specifically disclaim all responsibility for any liability, loss, or right, personal, medical, or otherwise, which is incurred consequently, directly, or indirectly, of the use and application of any contents of this book.
LLF Reads has allowed this work to remain exactly as the author intended, verbatim, without editorial input.

When ordering this title,
use ISBN: 9781737912071
PUBLISHED BY LLF Reads
www.lalafaithfulmd.com
Printed in the United States of America

BEGINNING PRAYER

In all thy ways acknowledge Him, and He shall direct your path.
Proverbs 3:6

My Father, My Father, I thank You for this day. I thank You for Your Presence and Love. I Thank You for all that You have done, doing, and about to do. Help me with this fasting, My Lord. Give me the strategic wisdom and to remain in Your Will. This is for Your Purposes in mind and **The Glorification of Your Holy Name**. In Jesus name I pray, Amen.

NOTES

CONTENTS

DAY 1	6
DAY 2	11
DAY 3	15
DAY 4	20
DAY 5	25
DAY 6	30
DAY 7	35
DAY 8	39
DAY 9	44
DAY 10	49

DAY 1

"No one who conceals transgressions will prosper, but one who confesses and forsakes them will obtain mercy."
Proverbs 28:13

Before you start on your fast today, pray to God about the reason for your fast.

GOAL/REASON:

_____
_____

PRAYER TOPIC:

_____
_____

SCRIPTURE:

_____
_____

RESULTS:

_____
_____

KEEP A LOG OF YOUR DAY TO MAXIMIZE YOUR RESULTS

PRAY FOR MERCY. RECEIVE JESUS.

MEDITATE:
_____

SCRIPTURE-BASED ON PRAYER:
_____

HYDRATE W/WATER:
_____

PRAY:
_____

GIVE THANKS:
_____

BREAK YOUR FAST:
_____

SLEEP WELL:
_____

TIPS

DO NOT STOP. KEEP GOING!

1. REPENT OF ANY SIN

The Lord is Your Strength!

DAILY JOURNAL - JOT DOWN YOUR THOUGHTS, ENCOUNTERS, MIRACLES, ETC.

DAY 2

*For thou shalt worship no other god: for the Lord, whose name is Jealous, is a jealous God."
Exodus 34:14*

Before you start on your fast today, pray to God about the reason for your fast.

GOAL/REASON:

_____

_____

PRAYER TOPIC:

_____

_____

SCRIPTURE:

_____

_____

RESULTS:

_____

_____

KEEP A LOG OF YOUR DAY TO MAXIMIZE YOUR RESULTS

WORSHIP GOD

MEDITATE:
_____

SCRIPTURE-BASED ON PRAYER:
_____

HYDRATE W/WATER:
_____

PRAY:
_____

GIVE THANKS:
_____

BREAK YOUR FAST:
_____

SLEEP WELL:
_____

TIPS

DO NOT STOP. KEEP GOING!

2. GET INTO INTIMATE WORSHIP WITH YOUR KING OF KINGS, WHO IS JEALOUS OVER YOU.

The Lord is Your Strength!

DAY 3

"Create in me a clean heart, O God, and renew a right spirit within me."
Psalm 51:10

Before you start on your fast today, pray to God about the reason for your fast.

GOAL/REASON:

_____
_____

PRAYER TOPIC:

_____
_____

SCRIPTURE:

_____
_____

RESULTS:

_____
_____

KEEP A LOG OF YOUR DAY TO MAXIMIZE YOUR RESULTS

PRAY WITH A PURE HEART

MEDITATE:
_____

SCRIPTURE-BASED ON PRAYER:
_____

HYDRATE W/WATER:
_____

PRAY:
_____

GIVE THANKS:
_____

BREAK YOUR FAST:
_____

SLEEP WELL:
_____

TIPS

DO NOT STOP. KEEP GOING!

3. PRAY WITH A SINCERE HEART. ASK GOD FOR A CLEAN AND PURE HEART..

The Lord is Your Strength!

DAILY JOURNAL - JOT DOWN YOUR THOUGHTS, ENCOUNTERS, MIRACLES, ETC.

DAY 4

"Exalt ye The Lord Our God, and worship at His footstool, for He is Holy."
Psalm 99:5

Before you start on your fast today, pray to God about the reason for your fast.

GOAL/REASON:

_____

_____

PRAYER TOPIC:

_____

_____

SCRIPTURE:

_____

_____

RESULTS:

_____

_____

KEEP A LOG OF YOUR DAY TO MAXIMIZE YOUR RESULTS

SURRENDER TO GOD LAY THEM AT THIS FEET.

MEDITATE:
_____

SCRIPTURE-BASED ON PRAYER:
_____

HYDRATE W/WATER:
_____

PRAY:
_____

GIVE THANKS:
_____

BREAK YOUR FAST:
_____

SLEEP WELL:
_____

TIPS

DO NOT STOP. KEEP GOING!

4. PUT ALL OF YOUR WORRIES, ANXIETY, AND PRAYER REQUESTS AT HIS FEET.

The Lord is Your Strength!

DAILY JOURNAL - JOT DOWN YOUR THOUGHTS, ENCOUNTERS, MIRACLES, ETC.

DAY 5

"And all things, whatsoever ye shall ask in prayer, believing, ye shall receive."
Matthew 21:22

Before you start on your fast today, pray to God about the reason for your fast.

GOAL/REASON:

_____

_____

PRAYER TOPIC:

_____

_____

SCRIPTURE:

_____

_____

RESULTS:

_____

_____

KEEP A LOG OF YOUR DAY TO MAXIMIZE YOUR RESULTS

ASK & YOU SHALL RECEIVE

MEDITATE:
_____

SCRIPTURE-BASED ON PRAYER:
_____

HYDRATE W/WATER:
_____

PRAY:
_____

GIVE THANKS:
_____

BREAK YOUR FAST:
_____

SLEEP WELL:
_____

TIPS

DO NOT STOP. KEEP GOING!

5. ASK THE LORD YOUR SAVIOUR, JESUS CHRIST (GOD) FOR HELP.

The Lord is Your Strength!

DAILY JOURNAL - JOT DOWN YOUR THOUGHTS, ENCOUNTERS, MIRACLES, ETC.

DAY 6

"Fear thou not, for I am with thee; be not dismayed; for I am thy god I will strengthen thee; yea, I will help thee; yea I will uphold thee with the right hand of my righteousness."
Isaiah 41:10

Before you start on your fast today, pray to God about the reason for your fast.

GOAL/REASON:

_____

_____

PRAYER TOPIC:

_____

_____

SCRIPTURE:

_____

_____

RESULTS:

_____

_____

KEEP A LOG OF YOUR DAY TO MAXIMIZE YOUR RESULTS

HIS WILL.
HIS WISDOM.

MEDITATE:
_____

SCRIPTURE-BASED ON PRAYER:
_____

HYDRATE W/WATER:
_____

PRAY:
_____

GIVE THANKS:
_____

BREAK YOUR FAST:
_____

SLEEP WELL:
_____

TIPS

DO NOT STOP. KEEP GOING!

6. USE THE WORD OF GOD (BIBLE) TO KNOW HIS WILL (WHAT GOD WANTS TO DO OR HIS PLANS FOR YOU) AND PRAY FOR HIS WISDOM (WHAT HE HAS INSTRUCTED YOU TO DO OR THE METHOD HE HAS INSTRUCTED YOU TO CARRY OUT HIS PLAN). FOR GROWTH, JOIN A TRUE CHURCH WHERE JESUS IS THE ONLY GOD BEING WORSHIPPED!

The Lord is Your Strength!

DAILY JOURNAL - JOT DOWN YOUR THOUGHTS, ENCOUNTERS, MIRACLES, ETC.

DAY 7

"And Jesus said unto them; Because of your unbelief; for verily I say unto you; if ye have faith as a grain of mustard seed, ye shall say unto this mountain; Remove hence to yonder place; and it shall remove, and nothing shall be impossible unto you."
Matthew 17:20

Before you start on your fast today, pray to God about the reason for your fast.

GOAL/REASON:

_____

_____

PRAYER TOPIC:

_____

_____

SCRIPTURE:

_____

_____

RESULTS:

_____

_____

KEEP A LOG OF YOUR DAY TO MAXIMIZE YOUR RESULTS

FAITH

MEDITATE:
_____

SCRIPTURE-BASED ON PRAYER:
_____

HYDRATE W/WATER:
_____

PRAY:
_____

GIVE THANKS:
_____

BREAK YOUR FAST:
_____

SLEEP WELL:
_____

TIPS

DO NOT STOP. KEEP GOING!

7. JUST BELIEVE IN GOD AND HIS WORD (BIBLE). DO WHAT HIS WORD SAYS AND PATIENTLY WAIT ON HIM. ONCE YOU START THINKING ABOUT IT TOO MUCH, THEN DOUBT CAN COME INTO THE PICTURE.

The Lord is Your Strength!

DAY 8

"But let patience have her perfect work, that ye may be perfect and entire, wanting nothing."
James 1:5

Before you start on your fast today, pray to God about the reason for your fast.

GOAL/REASON:

_____
_____

PRAYER TOPIC:

_____
_____

SCRIPTURE:

_____
_____

RESULTS:

_____
_____

KEEP A LOG OF YOUR DAY TO MAXIMIZE YOUR RESULTS

PATIENCE.

MEDITATE:
_____

SCRIPTURE-BASED ON PRAYER:
_____

HYDRATE W/WATER:
_____

PRAY:
_____

GIVE THANKS:
_____

BREAK YOUR FAST:
_____

SLEEP WELL:
_____

TIPS

DO NOT STOP. KEEP GOING!

8. BE PATIENT. MAKE SURE YOU DO YOUR PART OF RECEIVING JESUS CHRIST AS YOUR LORD AND SAVIOR. KEEP PRAYING, FASTING, AND HAVE FAITH WITHOUT DOUBTING. HE WILL SHOW UP FOR YOU!

The Lord is Your Strength!

DAILY JOURNAL - JOT DOWN YOUR THOUGHTS, ENCOUNTERS, MIRACLES, ETC.

DAY 9

"May my enemies be covered with disgrace; may they wear their shame like a robe."
Psalms 109:29

Before you start on your fast today, pray to God about the reason for your fast.

GOAL/REASON:

_____

_____

PRAYER TOPIC:

_____

_____

SCRIPTURE:

_____

_____

RESULTS:

_____

_____

KEEP A LOG OF YOUR DAY TO MAXIMIZE YOUR RESULTS

SHAME THE ENEMY.

MEDITATE:
_____

SCRIPTURE-BASED ON PRAYER:
_____

HYDRATE W/WATER:
_____

PRAY:
_____

GIVE THANKS:
_____

BREAK YOUR FAST:
_____

SLEEP WELL:
_____

TIPS

DO NOT STOP. KEEP GOING!

9. REALIZE THAT THIS IS A WICKED WORLD. EQUIP YOURSELF WITH THE WORD OF GOD. STAY PRAYERFUL AGAINST YOUR ENEMIES AND SPIRITUAL ATTACKS. CALL ONTO GOD FOR HELP.

The Lord is Your Strength!

DAILY JOURNAL - JOT DOWN YOUR THOUGHTS, ENCOUNTERS, MIRACLES, ETC.

DAY 10

"But thanks be to God, which giveth us the victory through Our Lord Jesus Christ."
1 Corinthians 15:57

Before you start on your fast today, pray to God about the reason for your fast.

GOAL/REASON:

_____

_____

PRAYER TOPIC:

_____

_____

SCRIPTURE:

_____

_____

RESULTS:

_____

_____

KEEP A LOG OF YOUR DAY TO MAXIMIZE YOUR RESULTS

VICTORY.

MEDITATE:
_____

SCRIPTURE-BASED ON PRAYER:
_____

HYDRATE W/WATER:
_____

PRAY:
_____

GIVE THANKS:
_____

BREAK YOUR FAST:
_____

SLEEP WELL:
_____

TIPS

DO NOT STOP. KEEP GOING!

10. VICTORY IS YOURS THROUGH CHRIST, JESUS! REJOICE!! WHETHER YOU HAVE SEEN THE RESULTS TO YOUR PRAYERS OR NOT, JUST REJOICE!!! THE BATTLE IS ALREADY WON!

The Lord is Your Strength!

DAILY JOURNAL - JOT DOWN YOUR THOUGHTS, ENCOUNTERS, MIRACLES, ETC.

www.ingramcontent.com/pod-product-compliance
Lightning Source LLC
Chambersburg PA
CBRC092058200426
43209CB00067B/1868